I'M SCREAMING
FOR HELP
BUT ONLY
TO ME

AN UNEXPECTED DEPRESSION-
MY UNWANTED CHAPTER

LJP

authorHOUSE®

AuthorHouse™ UK
1663 Liberty Drive
Bloomington, IN 47403 USA
www.authorhouse.co.uk
Phone: UK TFN: 0800 0148641 (Toll Free inside the UK)
*   UK Local: 02036 956322 (+44 20 3695 6322 from outside the UK)*

Published by AuthorHouse 09/22/2020

ISBN: 978-1-7283-7933-3 (sc)
ISBN: 978-1-7283-7932-6 (e)

Print information available on the last page.

Any people depicted in stock imagery provided by Getty Images are models, and such images are being used for illustrative purposes only. Certain stock imagery © Getty Images.

This book is printed on acid-free paper.

My Depression Survival Dedication

This poem was the foundation of my survival

And with the help from others after I communicated

Prevented my suicidal graduation

Enabled expression of my depression through writing, then… through narration

Dedicated to anyone suffering behind their mask in a depression fixation

And to the souls who lost to depressions whispers and left this world too early… I'm so sorry

Once I asked for some listening ear's I received salvation

Nana & Grandad P without knowing anything helped save me

Dad I was unhappy with what you told me, but ultimately

you helped lift me… when I needed to see

Trish who I told with a secret wish she would enlighten

Stevie P, a thankyou… She didn't fail me

Big D & Matty I thank you unconditionally the first time I

expressed my issue you was there.. we shared

You showed me that people really do care

Ree you listened to me when my mind was imprisoned, damaged and not free

Honey Badger, Della, Jane & Georgie G

Took in everything I'd written when I was stricken and didn't judge

They all in their own way 100% supported me

And to my Mum from you I come, you never lost me I'm still here and I'll always be your son

And to Big Harry Huckstepp, my hero, big love and bless you forever

To anyone fighting their own depression battle

Please listen… depression can be dismantled

Come away from the dark

Ask for help

And step in to the light

Everyone you know would be begging you to fight

Never stop kicking

Never give in

And depression and its crew will never ever win

Pain uncontrollable

Pain intolerable

Pain unacceptable

Pain not to be shown

Pain to be hidden

Pain will be a smile to all

Show no pain / it's not acceptable

But I see, dream, and feel a way out

A release from this sensation

Is just a heartbeat lost

Although that pulse I still have I can't let be bossed … at any cost

At all times my heart is slumped, my head is pumped

And I'm not gonna lie / my next move is stumped

As I believe my soul is defunct

Shake your head/ and sort it out

Spread your anguish and let it out

But lips are sealed as I function in my languish portrayal of an amazing life

Just it's not as I lost my wife

Couldn't hold on when I should've

I lost sight of our love

I chased what I thought was right

You disappeared out of sight

Gone

Gone

Gone

Now bygone days to everyone

But not to me … two years to the day …

You've had nothing to say

All belief has gone as you left me to go play

I didn't fight

I just let you take flight

Now my head has its own plight

Gone

Gone

Gone

My head's withdrawing

As it follows my heart into darkness and solitude

My inner rage is feeding a blood feud

Feeding

Feeding

Feeding

There's an inner turmoil I must keep subdued

My Instagram life is everyone's interlude

When all I feel is totally devalued

Shake your head/ and sort it out

Spread your anguish and let it out

Plunged into a mindset of despair

And I'm fighting to keep me from disrepair

My head's broken

My heart's broken

My inner being can't be outspoken

Shake your head/ and sort it out

This is a man's world (Slogan)

Guess what?

Most are secretly heartbroken

With their pain unspoken

Scared to put their feelings into the open

My manliness disguises my loneliness

It really is a phoniness

Unceremoniously this fall

I can see reaping after me

Breathing is killing me

Screaming from my inner soul deep / but you don't see

It was my conceding

Your misleading

It all added to your fucking scheming

Please ... Special pleading

Push on and walk on / I did

Whilst all along I was cheated on

Somewhere by the grandest of swans

Just made me want to drop atom bombs

But with considered aplomb

L. J. P. was no longer your dream

Or part of your scheme

Just tough for me

You were totally my bloodstream

Now downstream

These feelings are more extreme

With this broken soul struggling to let off steam—

My whole being wants to scream

But son

Where's your self-esteem?

Shake your head/ and sort it out

But I need your help show me the route

I thought we were a team

I'm broken; I've lost my dream

But it's seem okay under everyone else's regime

Chin up/ Chest out, son

Just give me a shout

But please be strong

Don't let your depression bomb out

You'll fuck it up

If you wave it under your colleagues' snouts

It's okay

I'm just trying to blank it out

I raised it once

Never again will I let it out

It just felt like you wanted me … to leave it out

Not hang it out, or was it knock him out?

So guess what?

I've been using my head as a depression hideout

All because of her fucking horned pout

Heads gone

Heads gone

Heads gone

That's not me

It feels so wrong

As I become suicidal and headstrong

Because you're dancing to your new swan song

All I want now is to become fucking King Kong

And play along for so long

But what you did was so wrong

I thought our LOVE was lifelong

It is for me … you see

PLEA … who me … never thee

I simply agreed

Cos at that time I was emotionally carefree

But that isn't me!

I fucking loved turning that church key

Before year two was through a sudden shock

I was hit with the final decree

Fuck me

Fuck me

Fuck me

All because you said I was an absentee

Fucking Otley

I always trusted in our love

I didn't mean to give it a shove

Unintentionally disposed of

By your unconditionally cheating … impatient of!

You are underserving of

All this brain pain

I'm suffering … Love

Love

Love

Love

Hₐ

I'm currently so alive

Head first into a swan dive

All other people I deprive … outside

I think I'd be satisfied with suicide

I must apologise

I'm terrified and fuck …

These feelings won't subside

I'm living an alive disguise

Pushing out my sex drive

Pretending I'm twenty-five

Tinderella is this fella

Not yet met a Nigella

Tinder

Tinder

Tinder

Is my kindling

To a new cauldron of embers

Remembers, remembers

That feeling reinvented

What Love?

No Pain

Pain, unacceptable pain

My cranium contents tremor

That matter is totally my stressor

Don't think I have the endeavour

To get better

It makes me live in terror

I can't take it forever

Whatever!

Measures my tempers …never

Completed by errors I'm not clever

However—Zephyr

My turmoil will become the aggressor

As I rage with my blood pressure

Turns out you were the transgressor

Transgressor

Transgressor

Beggar

Sorry—Offender

Correction, fornicator, or perpetrator

Well this is my gesture

You become our homewrecker

All for your sexual pleasure

You entered a male-female-male refresher

Where you received some liquid measures

You succumb to osmotic pressure

Cubic measure

Pubic pleasure

I hope you feel better

You're all so fucking clever

Causing displeasure

Square measure

You got my surrender

Surrender

Surrender

Surrender

I quit, you broke me—oh, you broke me

Adjusting your awe

While you bust my jaw

I knew I must withdraw

Because you was lusting for, and I thought you'd resisted all

But your adventure was celestial

Which in the end disrespectful

And two years down the line … resentful

In my life it's monumental

Go fuck yourself

Yourself

Yourself

Yourself

Obsession

Oppression

Accession

No confession

Increased aggression

But kept in regression

Can't show expression

Internal skull session … leads to depression

Show no facial expression

Wait depression

Ssssssssshhhhhhhhhh

Dr Session

For depression

Shake your head, son

Sort it out

PS: Don't be open in your expression

Or we will show oppression

Can't talk about depression

Not even with L. J. P.'s profession

But to help have a session

Write in progression to enable escape

Not always the safest plan!

But Eddie Vedder's the man

He's straight out of Pearl Jam

She thinks she found a better man

I know deep down tho!

I'm a greater specimen

More certain not the only one

She's had better ones or two ooohhhh

6 June 2015

You became my queen

It was my dream

That wedding was a fucking scream

But your marriage thoughts were obscene

You put up an innocent smokescreen

Whilst force feeding me kerosene

With Vaseline used on your slot machine

You're just a milking machine

Loving that simple protein … huhhhh

Head bobbing like a pinball machine

It was always your dream

The cat that got the cream

I sit with four beds

Trying to keep off the meds

Ain't good for my head

Concoction to suppress the threads

Ricocheting around … don't tell the feds!

Daily battle is real

I so want to squeal out this pain

It's just becoming surreal

And I don't want to be that nutter

Who just can't get over

I'm desperate for the changeover …

Suffering

Excruciating

Hangover

Get over

Get over

Bounce back, they all say

You took it in a relaxed way

But inside my pain is juxtaposing

With the outward smile I'm proposing

My fucking life is decomposing

Excruciating

Excruciating

Self-diagnosing

Contemplating overdosing

This whole situation is instrumental

Accidental

Not been gentle

Fuck … I think I'm mental!

Headspace is too sentimental

Being crackers … SHIT

I must rebel

Rebel

Rebel

Rebel

This broken soul needs to yell!

Maybe spill red blood cells

As a final farewell

Mademoiselle

I'm manic in a panic

Feeling volcanic went and fucked a Hispanic

Across the Atlantic

And that love sank like the *Titanic*

Don't want to be megalomaniac

Satanic

I should be talismanic

Chest out/ Chin up …

Buttercup

As I begin to slide

God damn have I cried

Those tears still haven't dried

I'm losing my pride

Losing my marriage was an unexpected broadside

I'm now on an unenjoyable death ride

Without you by my side

When …

Will these feelings subside

I've been pushed to the wayside

Considering myself self-homicide

But people would be horrified

If I went forward and simplified

As my feeling intensified

Get me some sulphur dioxide

Assist my suicide

But I have too much pride …

Euphoric suicide

You're sick or thick

Take your pick

Run from it

Extra logic to prevent something tragic

Catastrophic … Psychotic could I do it … Barbaric

Where does your suffering reside?

Deep inside

I'm fighting to keep me Alive!

I want to survive

Mental nut is unforgiving

Day to day reliving my misgiving

Depression

I need a presence of mind to engage your foothold

Fucking behold

You shall not cry

Chest out/ Chin out

Shake your head

Your dandy blockhead

Not unsuccessfully read …

Head

Head

It's in your head … but mine's not

God damn it's in my heart

It's in my heart with every depressed unwanted beat

I'm still on my feet

Currently my mind's in a dead heat

Dark me can only see the demise of my upbeat Pete …

So this white meat is trying to compete

Asking to be sat in the merry seat

But my mind

It plays trick or treat

Fuck

Beat a retreat and pull the ejector seat

My depression is about to overheat

I need a body made of reinforced concrete

If I accidentally die that would be bittersweet …

I'd be meat

Dead meat

I'd be happy to meet ...

Shake your head, son

Chest out/ chin up

Chest out/chin up

You've got nothing to be down about

You'll soon be out and about

Uptown

Downtown

FFS you're down ...

That's it, nervous breakdown

I remember when I was down

No one can help

So don't dare ask

Depression's behind a mask

Could be a smile ... could be a laugh

Standing in rank and file

This military mentality

It's not worthwhile

Depression can be stockpiled

But can become a lifestyle

Or life hostile

Life ticks away like shadowing a sundial

Don't lose your sun ... come on

Shake your head

Depressions nearly won!

It's nearly won; your time will be done

But be a man, and don't freshen your depression ... put it back in

your head and have a deep in depression jamming session

Only you can fix your nut's discretion

Hold it in; you'll lose your profession

Guys at work can't deal with your weak depression

Expect a bull session

To gouge out your manly confession

Look at any bloke's facial expression

You'll see suppression

For generations been told

There is no depression are you mental

Please don't cut your forearm

Next stop!

Funny farm

Funny farm

Not so fucking funny

Farmed emotions held in a headlock stable

Sat on a nut ward, head's on an operating table

Bloody unstable

Bloody unstable

I'm so unstable

I'm battling the mortality table

It's cold to the touch

But my thoughts are double Dutch

A two-skin paper

Minus a clutch

Let them continue to fight and battle it out

Too much!

Just don't let it out

Sssssssshhhhhhhhh

Endure the pain

You should feel the gain

I can't … Help I'm insane

Hold on … take the strain

We're your family, and this is just a migraine

So refrain, refrain, refrain from what you proclaim

We've got a reputation to maintain

Remember

Tough is good

Tough is great

Packmen are strong, too strong to break

With your mental illness ensure discreetness

It ain't no sickness … Jesus

Shake your head, son

Shake your brain

We can't hear about your pain

Don't try to explain …

We expect your thoughts to be plain

So plain

So plain

So plain …

Is your name Pack?

Oh, Fuck counter-attack

Wait, I'm not on Prozac

I'll get back to my cul-de-sac

I'm running back

With my thoughts turned ivory black

Panic attack

Please no negative feedback

Deep in my mind

Asthma attack

I must get back

For a second I was side-tracked

Let me draw back ... and hide

This crackerjack Pack

Wish my depression would turnaround and retract

Hold on!

You earn a packet

Upper tax bracket

But still can't buy my mind a flak jacket

The way I'm heading it'll be straight, straight, straight

To Hell

I can feel a brainstem instability

Not expecting much curability

I'm weighing up the probability

If my actions would get acceptability

Volatility ... volatility

Depression needs some gullibility

Or corruptibility

Tax those thoughts like a government

On every visit deduct a percentage

Eventually put depression in a cage

Fight it with rage

Be engaged

Depression you will disengage

Before I become deranged

And probably rampage

I'm so afraid

Enslaved

Enslaved in my cowardice

Is it wrong I feel powerless

While depression devours us?

Please help me fight

Someone empower us

Empower us

Empower us

I need a stewardess

A guide … a light

I'm still in this fight

Cowardice consumes us

Fucks us

"Suicide"

It's the easy way out

I hear them shout

Depressed cowardice is hazardous

Becomes amorous with your thought process … listen

Life's characterless

Not glamorous

Depression is slanderous

Oi nutter, oi nutter

Oi nutter

Your mind's fucked

It's fucked … full of clutter

You became a complete scrubber, hugger, a two-way fluffer

This pain has had its beginning

Have I passed the middle?

Am I winning?

Don't understand anxieties' underpinning

I bet you fucks would all be grinning

If you knew I was at the bottom of my innings

End in sight

My end's in sight

Yeah, right …

Please let me FIGHT

My fists are strong

Can't bash you all day long

Except my depression is too headstrong

Twirling my sense of right and wrong

Come on head, fuck … play along

Let's just get along

Shake your head

You're heading headlong

Taking this fight head-on!

Thought my inner guard was strong

I was so wrong

So wrong

My depression is too headstrong

Headstrong

This depression is a samurai

Cutting

Slashing

Stabbing my thoughts

In a trained and controlled swordplay

This I need to slay

But I have no way

No guidance is entering the fray

Every day I hide at the café

To see people I don't know

Beating depression is child's play they say

All ingrained with a shake your head inlay

Help me walk away

No, Fuck it!

Run away

Anyway

Divorcee is not for me

But now there's no depression breakaway

Depression is like a bird of prey

Swooping talons drawn

Ripping out my good

Like slaying a fawn

Goliath beating David … How?

Swords of Hebron

This dark cloud has approached once before

L. J. P. was able to show it the door

Grabbed its neck like I was Thor

But get fucked

It's back to equal the score

One, one after the second leg

Please, I beg … Extra time

Will be mine … just

Need to grow a spine

And keep out of the drugstore

Plus the liquor store

I'd be uncared for

This writing is leading me to the diplomatic corps

I deplore

I was in uproar

But didn't even the score

And about her I don't give a fuck anymore

Mind keeps racing

Body keeps pacing

Shake your head, and shake it out

Depression is embracing

With suicide chasing

With suicide chasing

Fucking suicide is chasing

And there's no replacing

Just gotta keep facing

This good and bad interlacing

Interlinking

Fuck overthinking

Overthinking

These thoughts are overlapping

Depression is clapping

Good mind is scrapping

Keep up the fight

Shake your head

Slug it out

Round 3 … you can't beat me

This is my bout

Depression's finger is on the trigger

But all my will is fucking bigger

Was down in the second

Won't be beat in the third

Haven't you heard the new catchword?

Depression you're getting served

I just need your password

Cos you've lost my safe word

I scream safe word

I scream safe word

My thoughts are wayward

Again fuck

You got my good like a jailbird

It's fucking absurd

Dr referred …

What's the opposite word, FIREBIRD?

FIREBIRD

As my ghost word

I ain't daunted

Suicide wanted

Suicide wanted

Is it wanted?

Well it's being flaunted

Don't read this; I'll be reported

If they know

I'm immortally exhausted

My good is being hunted

Depression wants it dead

Feels it's tormented

Well fuck you D … try this for size

Exorcize … demon be gone

Exorcise … freeman, freeman, freeman

Exorcize … Able seaman ride out the storm

It's definitely an art form

Enable you to transform

But again

Depression is using chloroform

Removed dress code, uniform … bang, it's in your head

Wanting me dead

Extinguishing my life form

Suicide, don't you hide

Come along for the ride

We are almost at high tide

Your mind will be purified

Get rid of that thought …

You had a bride

You had a bride

But she had a bit on the side

Tasted her love

It was cyanide

Her secret affair was classified

L. J. P. who cried

And was brushed aside

Went and lived in a desert countryside

Camels and scorpions

Was All that was there

Oh, and a fucked-up ex-husband

With his broken soul to bear

Pretended he didn't care

So no one cared

Shake your head and get it out

Turkish and Sammy L helped your route

And piss heads are us, numbed the pain

Health lookouts … yes they were

Helped me get through cos I was rough

Suicide strikeout

Depression was just on stakeout

Good mind to be cut out

If I lose this battle, mind and body blackout

Can I give a shout-out?

Big D

Was always there for me

So was Hunty and the other three

No shake-your-head chatter

Only

Get some help to deal with matter

You matter

Life matters

Spin the depression platter

Let those destructive thoughts scatter

L. J. P., you're not a nutter

No, mate

Definitely not the latter

We are always here for a chatter

And I know all of this

But I feel on an uncontrollable life sentence …

Correction …

Suicide life … suicide life

Fucked-up thoughts cut like a knife

I'm realizing it ain't nice

To be precise

These suicidal thoughts are becoming my vice

But can't succumb to self-sacrifice

Mind must change

Bird of paradise!

One more roll of the dice

My mind is currently a mixed-up splice

Depression and good intertwined and linked

Like an anchor on a chain preparing to sink

Currently got the stop button on!

Holding the winch

Sanity not giving an inch

Please don't flinch

This mindset is under pressure

Pounds per square inch

Depression's throwing its jab

Good mind trying not to flinch

Up on the ropes

Encased in a depression battle clinch

Get back … Get back

Hypodermic syringe

Depression binge

I think I'm unhinged

If people read this

I know they would cringe

Don't mention the D, L. J. P.

Straighten your back

Head up … Chin up … Chest out

Be a man, don't let it out

You can't be weak and look to seek

Any help … Depression Yelp!

Sssssshhhhhh, quiet lad

Don't let people know you're sad

Wear your pain like an invisible cloak

But I'm not sure I can cope

I can't help but mope

I'm on a suicidal tightrope

Tightrope

Tightrope

I think its around my throat

Totally a slippery slope

Should be happy

Cape of good hope

But she was getting a consensual grope

While I tried to earn pay in an envelope

Writing days = Five

I'm just trying to survive

This unforgiving beast that's inside

Again, someone

Be my guide

But fuck, Len

You won't find no guide or way to survive

If you continue to hide

Come out from the dark side

Forget that cheating bride

She was never fully allied

To get over her will be like climbing a mountainside

And yes as we see

The path is fortified

But remember

Your suicide won't be glorified … in fact, probably denied

As family and cunts will be mystified

Why, why, why

Did he do it they would all cry

But I will only know the reason why

My mind feeling justified

Reason being classified

Do you think I could actually use cyanide?

Cut myself … side to side

Dive into acid become liquefied

Swing from a tree

My neck all tied?

Or more fitting to my demise

Take an Orwell Bridge Swan dive

Swan dive

Swan dive

Do you think that would be something I'd survive?

What are the odds?

I'd be backing God's hands

But suicide … I'd be meeting the devil's dogs

Devil dog's

This would be my price level … dancing with the devil

But nothing new to my suicidal awareness

Death Boom … Here I come, the Prince of Darkness

Amazing depression

Stripes your sharpness and your hardness

Don't show it no weakness

Open your eyes

It's the crucifier

Lucifer

The executioner

Step outside; let's have a straightener

This round three … good is a latecomer

But let me remind you I'm definitely a competitor

For too long now I've been on the side lines

Had no will to fight

But now is the right time

An up an at 'em approach

Introducing

Ladies and gentlemen

The challenger

He's a newcomer

Hold up, wait

Are you ready L. J. P.?

Or are you already beat

Depression is rock steady

Things are about to get heavy

It's a brutal bomber

Top yourself you'll be calmer

But there will be no honour

Only an overwhelming shame

Disgrace

Dishonour

People won't understand he had so much Dollar

Followed by a pause, a breath, a comma

Question yourself:

Do we do enough for the ones we love

Or do we fall short of true love?

Sort of

Sort of

I'm trying to swim wearing boxing gloves, gumshield, and pads

I thought it was love

Heavens above

Bubba, you've gone

My will to succeed helped me to get it wrong

I see now that quickly those blokes could catch on.

And from that moment on you went

Secret liaison

Self-guide for Depression

Good heavens … shit

First one I look at, moodjuice.com

It's exactly me—

Sad/Low/Flat … Tick

Tearful shhhhh

Don't let people see

Shake your head/ don't let it out

But it says behaviour patterns

Fuck, I'm reading my life out

And all are describing me

Fuck me

Fuck me

See … Self-diagnosis was easy

Got it

You're crazy

And it's making you lazy

These depressing thoughts are murmuring

Massaging your brain in a destructive way

Good side of L. J. P. … yield … give way

Depression submitting is easy

But admitting,

Admitting not so

How do you know your brain is on go slow

Do mentally ill people actually know

I seek out the cure

And seek some respite?

But all I see is my imminent demise

Why're my thoughts like this I thought I wise

That cunt of depression pops up like Pennywise

Think my balloons are deflated like my insides

Heartbreak is real

And if left unchecked

Is an out-of-control Ferris wheel

Mind neglect

Have FFS some self-respect

You do this, lives will be wrecked

Depression and suicide is a touchy subject

But I'm trying to listen but can't

It's in a Cantonese dialect

Flipping heck

Please help me correct

Don't want any tablets

They won't work or take affect

Broken heart is my diagnosis

Twisted like my back, scoliosis

These suicidal thoughts creep back

Fuck, harden up … you're a Pack

Shake your head … Why you in bed?

Stand tall … Take hold of the ball

And take this final by the scruff of the neck

Unleash your fury but don't let people see

You're just being silly so …

Man up!

Who me? Okay

Conscious suicide

You decide

Do it today?

No way

Nest week?

Let me think

Mind now like a melting ice rink

One false step your life has gone

Turn it down to zero

Freeze it back hard

Be your own hero

Hero

Hero

Superhero

Depression is my kryptonite

Good mind come on join this fight

Backbite … Right

Be the white knight

Learn to fight

Keep your head

Beacon of light

Everything is gonna be alright

Use anything you can, a candle?

Come to the light

But which way is that?

Forward or back

In certain minds

That's a proxy fight

Depression, guess what? You're a parasite

Something I need to overwrite

Then get the patent right

Shake your head …

And what?

Be alright

Don't get to the burial site

Do the crackerjacks know their fate

Or just wander in a doped- up state?

Forward march they say

Towards suicide's open gate

Who's with me?

Anyone,

Mate?

Readers of this

There will be a few

Couldn't really let my feelings out

Thought of that is making me spew

Spew my sense of pride

Remember

Depression you must hide

People will say I would have helped

But normally when it was too late

'Why didn't he talk to his family or me' they will cry

Probably he was told to Man-up a few times

So he decided to hide

Look in deeper at that unhappy smiler

He's hiding his fear from all to see

That half-scared bloke feels everything

Too scared to heal his head

In full expectation

Of being dead

Attention

Attention

Attention please

Depression portrayed as a shameful stigma

Shown probably at suicide

When that bloke is dead

Then what

Pow … enigma

This suicide is a headscratcher

Brain-teaser

Braun tester

Can't decipher

He had so much charisma,

But depression was his guerrilla

Guerrilla warfare

It isn't fair

It's in my head

Depression hits and runs

My good is becoming overrun

Camouflaged from all around

But depression uses sabotage

It's now at large

Bringing all its entourage

Anxiety, fear a be afraid idea

Then can be concealed with sleep,

Sleep

Sleep

Do I really sleep?

Maybe just lie, laying there counting sheep

Uncontrolled depressed emotion

I've hidden it except it's becoming a real notion

Silhouetted in my spare room state

Boxes here open with all to bear

Don't look too deep

You'll see my glorious suicide

Glorious to no one

Except depression… it's still in my head

Lurking and skulking

Manhandling my good

Fightback concealed

All my thoughts are congealed

Tread carefully, fucker, minefield

All will be revealed

I could become exposed; let's go

Battlefield

Depression AND suicide

Hand in hand

Magnetic field, two wrongs collide

Outcome equals

Pain … Oh Fuck

Disqualified

I'm a depression dweller

Didn't realise a storyteller

Keep it up it will be a bestseller

A helper

A sharer

A bloke living in terror

A self-killer depression wishes I was

A fortune teller

Let me help you, fella

It'll be my pleasure

Mind's like a shuffled deck

But guess what?

It's a wreck, yeah cunt, a wreck

Thought I was a roughneck

Problem is my thoughts are at a bottleneck

I lost it all for a pay cheque

Disability check

Binge thinking

Broke thoughts are really fucked

Desperately dancing with depression

My mind needs a flammability test

Testing

Testing

Come on, let's get it addressed

We can't believe you're depressed

You commit suicide there will be an inquest

He became suppressed

Swimming in his thoughts, depressed

Help him please

Fuck no life vest

Top yourself is only self-interest

But I feel second-best

And if I feel any worse, strap on that bulletproof vest

Will it protect my chest

Worn under my Sunday best?

Survival instincts outkicked

Packy boy's struggling to win

Depression's trying to smuggle in a gun

Quick, L. J. P., run, hide, tell, tell someone

Tell who … you?

Fuck you … This is my battle

I come alone

Depression wants to cut me to the bone

Wear a crown and sit on your thrown

Good mind lies prone

Your family will disown

When you're under the headstone

Depression

It's just a stepping stone

Can't lie, this is my biggest opponent

Guard's up

Defending every component

Stay in the moment

Keep your eye on the ball

Stay in the moment

Don't dare to blink

Your amazing persona will fucking sink

Only comes good with help, Corona

Corona … Corona

Take a sip, Pack Cruyff out of your feet

Shot's on!

Barcelona to Benidorm

Ha no chance

Depression be gone

Make your own luck

Mind treads water in shark depressed fluids

They circle my good like psychotic druids

Stonehenge … Head-unhinged

Depression needs a sacrifice, an offering

Suicide slut

Ensure the knife is deeply cut

Deeply cut

Deeply cut

Look at the pain

Look at the pain

Ain't got no strength

Flex my muscles to scare the opponent

Depression just laughed

Fuck me Packy

Your late-night thoughts you're wacky

I need to get my crew to fight

Including my insight, strength, guile

Pride, a will to survive

These members I beg don't leave my side

Or leave me behind

Depression hounds snap at my heels

I should of insisted Court of Appeal

Instead I just went carb-free meals.

Glucose starved thoughts depression would divide

Maybe collapse like a house of cards

But maybe herbs

You know … In other words

Drugs to mask the depression

In a cage deep inside

You top yourself Pack

You'll be the black sheep

It's a hell of a drop

It's Fucking steep

Better to strap it up

And go balls deep

Then onto REM sleep

Dreaming of Night Swimming

But constantly Tindering women

My inbox is brimming

I'm not kidding

Keep changing my bed linen

I want to be forgiven

I feel like a fake

A dating villain

100 per cent was not my mission

But neither was self-killing

Still don't know how

But the concept is chilling

I'm sure some cunts would be grinning

If I made that decision!

Question

Is suicide classed as sinning?

I've never tried, and this continues to be an uncomfortable ride

Let me tell you all something

I've been taking finasteride

Maybe identified if others have tried

Seems depression could be its unpleasant side

Honesty

Pride

Often I've cried

And I've felt terrified

Since I lost my wedded bride

Afterlife

I watched alone and cried

Tony, Gervais character, was lonely

His wife had died

I was by his side

I could relate to his loss

No one really gives a toss mine wasn't dead

Just upped and left

As the mornings pass

My mourning intensifies

Don't let no one see you cry

Think you should die … Cries

Depression out of my head

This grief is now real in everything I feel

So please someone help my good survive

Depression will thrive

Is anyone on my side?

This is not a comic vine

Help me realign

This can't be my time

Depression tells me there's a deadline

What?

Get it

Deadline …

No please define

Give me more time

I'm in an earthquake

And my mind's on the fault line

Ring this number, nutter

Suicide Hotline

Keep your mind online

Don't resign to depression

Sinn Fein versus the oppression

Once you cross the white line

It will be your time

No ninety minutes have been assigned

A battle for your life

To stop it from unwinding

Like a school massacre

Columbine

Them poor kids deserved their lives

And you're contemplating snuffing yourself out

You selfish cunt

Can I be blunt?

Having your life is like a treasure hunt

But listen please

Currently a battlefront

Depression vs. Life

Now see my strife

I feel like I need to unsheathe my knife

And yes, others have a right to life

Depression attacks though

Feel those thoughts spread

Butter knife

Spreading my thoughts into the afterlife

Adultery is rife

From a lot we call housewife

Seeking eternal life

With a new set of nuts

Whhhhaaatttt?

She coverts nuts like an English grey squirrel

Before you realise it, your marriage is in deferral

Can your heart have an epidural

If you don't mow your lawn

Then someone else will

Now that just wants to make me go kill

But still if you don't want my side

Thank fuck, get fucked go untied

I won't beg you … you hear

You turned out mental yourself

Jekyll and Hyde

And if I'd begged

I'd have lowered myself

Been undignified

Let me point something out

Affair accentuation to me

You cunt, unjustified

I valued my marriage

Like the queen's gold carriage

But your cheating

Was a marriage miscarriage

Wedlock to me

Was giving and taking

I had an end goal in sight

It was there for the shaping

What you did was degrading, degrading

Degraded

Degrading depression

Embarrassed I feel

Still! Like a failure

And I don't know why

Felt I was hung out bare-assed to cry

I wasn't a diarist

Back then

I let my pain build up

Weighed heavy on my brow

You could see it in my frown

Not talking has put Packy

In the Danger Zone

My mind is in two different time zones

Struggling present

And mourning the past

Neither is pleasant

Fuck no

Torment,

Torment

Tormented I bet you all laughed

Well I'm doing my best

Grave accent

Get passed

Antidepressants

Open those little presents

Guess our wedding was your hidden weapon

I'd never have dreamt you was that unpleasant

But no getting around it

YOU'RE A C…

Shall we have a punt executive vice president?

Yep you're still a c…

Depression-flavoured life

Divorce has become a real uncontrolled strife

I understand now

Your cheating was rife

Two shaking hands clasping the knife

Thrust in my heart

Eternal life

But listen L. J. P.

You're great

Right to life

Park those thoughts

Hide your anguish

We'll get you right, quality of life

Woke up at seven

No emotion to question

Wait, did I really dream of a life in heaven?

Oh yeah … again

Seven days straight

Seventh visit to heaven this week

Makes my heart heave

And it's now what I'm starting to believe

I Scream

A silent scream

Depression-flavoured ice cream

Thawing and melting through my fingers

Like my lost zest for life

Christ

Where's that gone?

Let's get it back

It's my quest,

It's my quest

But life wait …

I have a request

Help me

To be my best

I want to stand tall

Pride all across my chest

But with these destructive anxious thoughts

I can feel it

I'm distressed

So I must remember

Shake your head, son

Chin up … Chest out

Keep your anguish for another year

Let me be clear

We will deal with it if it ever reappears

To the world welcome

My depression premieres

You're welcome to the freak show

But this mind isn't all it appears

Roll up,

Roll up

But I dare not speak

This written account is my life compere

Hidden under Fox flex fit headgear

I'm worried I'm losing my career

I'm in safety … racketeer

I keep you safe

But don't protect your mind

I've been invaded by a cuckoo named crisis

It's left its egg of depression

For my life to raise

Within my mind

Until it's time to overpower humankind

That time is approaching

Crisis is encroaching

Isis caliphate in my state of mind

Hold up, please

Rewind

I'm struggling

Indecisive mind

Jump off the bridge

No, hold up

I'm still deciding to live

Look at depression

Help me, can I vaccinate?

I need to use my good mind and assassinate

The growing mind of the caliphate

Protect

All of me that was great

That's right great

I used to be such a great guy

Eye's as blue as the sky

But darkened and dulled

As crisis encases my skull

I can feel the pull

As depression masticates my will to live

To validate the conflict in my mind

Two steps forward

Hoping to find,

Find,

Find what?

My inner being screams out

Have you not listened you lout?

My time is almost out

Time slips away

Day after day

L. J. P. is busy dying but is outwardly lying

That mask is on

It smiles to everyone

Back to how a man should be ... don't look at me

I can't tell you my mind isn't free

Free

Depression imprisons me

And at this exact moment it's holding the key

L. J. P. just wants to be set free

Free to live

Free to thrive

But hold up

Depression doesn't want you to survive

Feel free to dive

Swan dive it's back in my mind

I think he committed a crime

Please depression fuck off

Give me more time

I keep telling you

Listen

I want to survive

Be alive

Not get by

I mean depression be gone

I don't even want you in quarantine

Because we would reconvene

Back on the depression time machine

My heart is heavy

My head is unsteady

Seven kgs of depression and crisis

My neck and my body can't take it

Soon I'll be lifeless!

Depression at its finest

High price to pay your highness

Browbeats you down into your lowness

My yin and yang

Have a situation

My good mind is going through dislocation

A separation from the normal thinking

I'll say it again

I'm fucking sinking

In danger of totally overthinking

Then overreacting

Considering downsizing

My house

My car

My entire being

Does this mean death?

You decide

But let me tell you this

Depression is determined I die

Keeps telling me I'm a burden

A McDermott servant

Daddy's little observant

And when people say that I can't help it …

I'm squirming

Things like that just add to my hurting

I stand with the world at my feet

Looking out

Wishing my mind had more clout

Stricken in my thoughts

Depression not letting me out

Or even shout … anything …

My mentality is in a downswing

I struggle to grin or even smile

It's truly been a while

I'm deep in a depression pool with a blocked snorkel thing

Ever since I put on that wedding ring

Or …

Was it when I took it off!

I don't fucking know; I'm totally lost

See I've said it again

Is it my left brain or right

That is winning this fight?

Cyprus Hill was right

Insane in the membrane

Insane in the brain

Again I'm on the depression train tonight.

My mind is in chains

Uncontrolled pain

Told depression is no excuse

Your anguish you must hide

So lately

I keep people away

I sit writing on my stool

My mind a tangled spool

Exercise is a distant memory away

Kept me sane

Should have kept it up

My life is going down the drain

Sanity juices again

This divorce

Keeps giving abuses

And my inner brain is suffering bruises

Depression introduces

Body and mind misuses

I can't face it on my own

But it was the way I was grown

Face it totally alone

Suicide sushi as raw as I condone

This non-verbal ability

Totally homegrown

Totally homegrown,

Homegrown

You're on your own

You don't really belong

You'll be okay, son

You're headstrong

PS, your mother has gone

She was always the underdog

And God bless her

Now she hunts the hair of the dog

This digital world has passed her by

Like her son I know she cries

And like him

Her mind is in backlog

Of what life has been

A fucking slog

An only child I will always be

Five younger half siblings who don't really know me

All I feel want a competition as a test

To prove they can be better than L. J. P.

My nana and grandad

Raised me

I love them dearly

All can see

I'm now crawling my own road

Depression calling

But they won't let me go

Thank God they are here

Cos I know

I would totally disappear

Depression buccaneer

Crisis puppeteering

Fighting to get out

How?

William Shakespearing

Young boy in a wheelchair

He had that vacant stare

And I tried not to look; may I dare?

He was in a movable armchair

His mum providing childcare

And in that split-second

I lost my despair

It fucked off elsewhere

My heads back and forth

Like a rocking chair

He had it rough

But he looked so damn tough

My inner good wanted to give him a celebratory fist pump

My life can't be as bad as that little fighter's

I suddenly felt brighter

Realised I was launched by a fucking speed hump

I felt for that little blighter

I actually shook my head and had a word

With my inner writer

I explained that depression

It's the toxic ignitor

The Rough Rider

The fucking horned viper

Let's not be a monthly subscriber

It just makes me sadder

Like I'm climbing a burning Jacob's ladder

And depression waiting for me to fall

Like a curled-up death adder

Will attack my gray matter

Cerebral cortex

I'm in a depression vortex

Remove from my brain

Use forceps in accordance

To prevent suicidal rigor mortis

Need this depression removed

Like an abortus

But missed that chance

It's fucking way too enlarged

I'm oxygen starved

This suicide is reserved

Is it deserved?

You need some fucking nerve

Suicidal thoughts are ravenous

My life is malnourished

It's famished

I'm haemorrhaging my life

But I don't let people see

I'm begging for help but only to me

If only people could realise

L.J.P's mind is brutalized

Bullied bad

Bullied by its own

Should heal mentality

Be unsullied

Clean of this depression abnormality

It swings with brutality

Stifling my joviality

Clouding my rationality

Becoming a suicidal speciality

Looking down on myself

Virtual Reality

Developing a psychopathic personality

Callously

But only in my own fantasy

To kill me

I'd be the only casualty?

Wouldn't I?

If I die

I'm enrolled … first term

Suicide academy

Is it insanity?

I'm a self-examinee

Head filled with depressed profanity

Fuck remember

Your family

They'd all be casualties

And I want to tell them

But I'm struggling with a be tough vanity

The words are stuck in my thoracic cavity

Held in with depressed agony

Perform an emergency tracheotomy

Let my breath be free

I want to talk openly

But you'll think I'm mental

Dr Prefrontal Lobotomy

Slice that mind

Wait for the volcanic mudslide

A tidal wave … tsunami of pain will ensue

Fuck you,

Fuck you,

Let's join the suicide posse

All because you became an Omani

As for help join the illuminati

Attack depression … how?

Karate

Freemasonry will help

Show you the way

Secret handshake will defeat

The depression agency

Save your life; don't be wasteful

I hear you say

Suicide has no graceful way

But we need a vigorous regulatory agency

As speculation grows

It can only be said

Only L. J. P. knows

Anxious and dangerous thoughts

Enter my free mind space

I want to tell the press agency

But been trained

Defend myself

Until I'm black and blue

Come on people

You must have a clue

I want to tell you; I really do.

Painfully I suppress the truth

But patiently bide my time

Until my loved ones have gone

And then

I can fill my suicidal vacancy

No such thing as a blameless suicide

There's always a trigger

And if it's held down tight enough

The situation gets bigger

Need to steady your mind

Deploy the outriggers

Fragility of thoughts

Suicide hair trigger

I'm so worried I can hear people snigger

I'm so quick to backbite

Ready to fight

But not in my mind

Hold it all in all right

Heads full of air … bagpipe

People always think, *L. J. P.*

Your sweetness and light

Not realizing your head's fucking cooking

100 degrees Fahrenheit

Depression fight

Depressed in this fight

Pack, keep your lips sealed

Airtight

Accidental fatality

Is stalking me

I think it's an abnormality

Death this way is just a technicality

A prayer for a conventional death

Is still a suicidal fatality

You won't be free

Just a dead unwanted divorcee

Top yourself, Pack

You, Judas Machete

You'll never make it to be a retiree

If people knew you'd get the third degree

Count down or count up

Could I hang from a tree?

I keep asking me

Would people visit L. J. P.'s execution tree?

Take me to my lowest degree

But my putty mind would be free

Things could be worse

How L. J. P.?

I wouldn't wish this on you … What?

You wouldn't want me to be

Lonely,

Lonely

Always with people but always alone

Have no one to do nothing with

Just my battling mind

It's under attack

I need to push back

Ask for caller ID

Please show me

Don't give a fuck if you disagree

I'm the divorcee

Devotee

You held the control key

Fuck me … Fuck me

Apache attack

Depression Cherokee is currently mind-scalping me

Depression wants to charge an entrance fee

You can guarantee

People will cry

He should of asked me

But what do I say; help my poor head

Problem is

I think I'm insane, crackerjack, brain dead

Get more vitamin D; that'll help thee

Become more happy

I'm sorry to say though, that isn't me

I'm so long-term unhappy

Let me recce a tree

That's big enough for me

Be easier if I was dealing with homosexuality

In Barcelona … Mediterranean Sea

You want to bum me

Poppers you see, I mean smell

That situation would just add to your hell

Depression could not be more …

Suicidally complementary

It's the easy way out

It'll take you to heaven

Lie slain in a coffin

There … you're the skeleton key …

Don't forget though, deaths depression docking fee

You may disagree but we know

Your mind's full of debris

I'm writing this book on my depression

A good referee

Relieve me

Unshackle me

I want to be footloose and fancy free

Please fancy me

Inside I hear me plea

To any lady who will look at me

But my love receptor is obstructed

I need it liberated

But I was raised antiquated

Depression is understated

You must fix yourself

Be a man; don't be deflated

All the family and society dictated

Scared to speak out

Of being castrated

Need my free speech and happiness to be located

Before suicide is detonated

Then and only then will all be devastated

This feeling is not fabricated

Daily my mind is inundated

Isolated

Soon to be terminated

But will I be back

Mind repopulated?

I felt I was emasculated

If I hang from a tree I worry I will be decapitated

If I die keep me refrigerated

I could share out my organs

But not L. J. P.'s heart; it's damaged

Incapacitated

Broken in two

Degraded and wasted

If the rest is usable

Please and the bits aren't tainted

Share out my lungs and give another a better life

If you share out my mind, I'm sorry there's a built up hatred waiting

It's tainted

Totally degraded

Bury that part so it can become reacquainted

With the earth and the worms

I dreamt I'd be sainted

But depression has me now

It's complicated

I'm contaminated

Struggling on my own

To be rehabilitated

In fact

I feel totally deflated

Depression sets the trap

Yep it's been baited

Relax L. J. P., keep ventilated

Attention to detail

Don't become self-terminated

Suicide of L. J. P. would be unsubstantiated

He wouldn't do that unless premeditated

Definitely intoxicated

To top himself man

Currently in a fight with depression

Trying to stop himself

Suicide, damn

But he was a good man … Was he?

Ask yourself, did you do all that you can?

There are two people alive

Who prevent my suicide

It would tear them inside

I don't think they would survive

So I continue a depression battle

Overdrive

It would be a cunt's act … surprise

Be like I was committing genocide

And I'd have no way to apologise

With the rest of my family I'd of died

But I'd be totally despised

Despise,

Despise

I despise myself

But I put on a depression disguise

So it can fucking hide

Allows me to pretend to get by

Before I say my goodbye

How would people reply

If they realised

That depression is taking over?

I thought it would pass over,

Like locusts fly over.

Let me tell you cunts not much good is leftover

A total depression takeover

Should I go to the doctor's

Get a once over

A mental mind medical

Pretend I'm okay behind my depression -filled mask?

Don't dig too deep, Doc, it's a grim task

You'll see my depression grinning back

Telling you all that suicide is a willed act

L. J. P.

Fight back

You've slipped back

And you're under attack

Lost your mind's grid map

Pass us map

Please L. J. P. come back

Your mind's cells are taking flak

I'm trying

But I've had another setback

What a load of crap

Stop fucking bareback

Empty the tank

You're blindfolded on depression's dangerous gangplank

Fuck it

Let's go into armoured combat

Strategically strap up

Don't be silly

Conscious scrutiny of everything that is me

My depression's leading a life mutiny

Hopefully, fruitlessly … honestly

I know suicide is lunacy

Leave a tip

Gratuity

Tinder and Bumble promiscuity

Forward I step with depression

Blinkers each side

Shielding my sight

Of the life I have … right

I say this all truthfully

Gloriously … suicide

Mysteriously touts to me

Beckoning me to come join thee

Notoriously it's McGregoring me

I'm down on one knee

Pleading to be let free

Depressive—that's currently me

It needs to leave me

To let my future be progressively

Better than it is

Get over this it will be impressive

My normal mind has gone non-aggressive

Equals ... non-progressive

Depression is so suppressive

Its incessant ... a constant

And its little niggles are so suggestive

Becoming a total mental menace,

Mental menace

I'm playing mental mind table tennis

Do you think I'm jealous

Or just heartbroken and sad?

Desperation

To survive this suicide fetish

I've not googled that search

I know the results will fucking hurt

Not something I want to see

I know suicide would be beckoning me

Apprentice Mr L. J. P.

Penance is what I want from thee

Go hang from that tree

Then all would see

Your acceptance to follow suicide

Tick in the box

We've checked your attendance

I sit in my kitchen

Writing this lot

When all of a sudden I hear *BANG* ... gunshot

Turn my head to see

The summer fat pigeons flying; they flee

I for a split-second wish that bullet had hit me

Then I begin to see

Maybe depression has taken someone before me

I will have to wait and see

If a suicidal comrade has made it to heaven

Shit … where would they actually go?

Does anyone know?

Knowing my luck, down below

Fornicating with the devil

Before decaying

Once down there no normal mating

Or communicating

FFS Len, shake your head

Storm abated

I'm not 100 per cent sure when I started hating

At my divorce? Nah uncorrelated

There's been an underlying brew circulating

It's just been on hold … again call waiting

I've unknowingly answered that call bollock, fuck damn

Now

Depression, anxiety and hate are placating

And by fuck now they are dominating

Don't tell anyone, Pack, it's degrading

Do I go see a counsellor?

Hell no

But I've heard it's liberating,

Liberating,

Liberating,

Occupying force has me on a collision course

And to myself I cannot lie

At least twice a day I want to cry,

Cry,

Cry,

Cry baby cunt

Don't you realise your mind is a delicate bonsai?

To many people to say goodbye

I honestly thought I was a good guy

Tell you what

Funeral black tie

I know some fuckers' tears would be bone dry

The love of them to me is calcified

Mummified … now a wrinkly bride

But if I do derail the train

To end my pain

I must change quick my insurance pay-out

That cunt's on the list

Her amount would be way out

She could live for free and days out

Swan feathers cover her body

Splays out

If she received that cheque

Guarantee pass out

Open her bank up

Cash out

Kerching,

Kerching

My suicide would be far-reaching

But would anyone really miss me?

I'd fall in the abyss

Davey Jones locker I'd be kissing

I suddenly read afterlife two to proceed

Gervais, you legend, this is something I need

I hope it helps me succeed

I really plead help my saddened mind pulp

Please be freed

I think take two will help save me …

If I come through this battle with my mind not totally unravelled

And I'm still in the saddle

Fucking yeeeharrr

You were able to grapple

And wrestle and fight

Lift up your spirits … How?

I used a block and tackle

Now if you reach an open-minded channel

Don't let depression come back or rappel in

You'll be back in the dogfight

Depression doesn't have to have the bigger bite

Duelling minds at dawn thoughts will fight

Today I woke up and straight to the café

Scramble, bacon, cheap pork sausage left out the hash

Something's different

Feeling a little more courage

Today … be brave

Don't let depression become depraved

What shall I do?

I know; be an escaped depression hostage

That's it, yes escape this depression bondage

A suicidal homage

Let's forget this depression blockage

I'm Fucking L. J. P. now acknowledge

Today I shook my head

Leapt out of bed with a drive

To survive

I actually feel alive

Good thoughts in overdrive

Satisfied I won't think of suicide

To depression I won't apologise

Just stand tall, chest out, chin up, and shook my head

Languish is out

I understand today the importance of life

Been jamming to Monster Florence

Keep it on, Chilli Chilli what a performance

A complete suicidal deterrence

With this L. J. P. is back for a reappearance

Oh my God I still ain't sold out

Day 8 has been great

I had lots to help me escape

Woke up at 3 a.m.

Thunder crashing outside my window

Enabled me to rise feeling more wise

Spent the day with Big D

It excited me that for that one day

I was depression -free

Suicidal tide had subsided

Washed away; let's hope for longer than a day

Hooray

Spent the evening at Woodbridge Town FC heaven

Lots of reliving

Old friends I thought wouldn't remember me

But did you see?

Had an extremely good laugh

Helped my mental mindset get right

Amazingly felt right overnight

Don't want a depression fright

This writing gives me insight

And Mr Fosker added some guidance for me that night

Some preparation to fight

And I started to head for the light

Today is day 9

And I actually feel fine

Well at this precise time

Head's mind has wrestled with grime

No longer at suicide's shrine

Four beers in

Love it

See you tomorrow, Pedro

For two weeks now

Since I felt enlightened

I've been dancing with depression

Things, attitude, and life have been brightened

Although, There's an underlying worry

I'm still afraid

Salsa dancing daily with a suicidal quickstep

I wasn't sure but I began to believe

I didn't need help

But scheming suicide again

Approaches my side

Arrived in Milan

I'm back in pain

Depression is back; it's been turned on

Stretching its arms, embracing me … its wingspan

So fucking large

Got me like the boogeyman

I'm again its leading man

But don't want to be extinct … Mastodons, they're all gone

I traipse to work every day

Like a company man nine to five

Head's like a Neanderthal

Abdominal strain all from my heart's broken charts

This depressed brain

Outwardly feigns to all its inward intention

Its pain

You're insane

I'll fill your head with a depressive gain

You can't block the pain

We are going for a blood–brain drain

It's again depression's campaign

Slip the rope

Champagne, Champagne for everyone

Your life is now uncontrollably mundane and it's made your mind slip

Mental terrain

Are you insane?

These constant thoughts are now your ball and chain

It doesn't matter you've been on a gravy train

Eating quiche Lorraine

Let's cut me deep

Femoral vein

Then all your suffering will be in the public domain

Everyone on a whispering campaign

Detain depression

Straight into confinement

Outward persona publicly aligned

Keep quiet you

Want to swallow a M4 Carbine

But I'm on a deadline

Mind again in decline

I feel I'm gonna stick it over my own goal line

Suicide hotline

Every day I step over the landmines

Landmines of my mind

It's off the mainline

I keep showing it the V sign

I want to resign

My mind is again on the bottom line

Or is it the firing line

Soothe my pain … Calamine

Depression, though, has a direct line

Transmission all around my matrimonial vine

What a joke

That's depression's masterstroke

To provoke

A constant slowpoke

Hides under a poisonous cloak

Encouraging a suicide that's bespoke

Neck wrapped with a rope—choke

Could you be that bloke?

Remember we've already spoke

And yes, you're broke

Your heart's been beat, egg yolk

You're holding it in … powder keg

I know my inner good is trying to beg

Open my eyelids to this depression falsehood

Your losing your manhood

You must be misunderstood

Again depression's on a takeover bid

And its gonna cost you your livelihood

You're good

A sainthood

But my mind's broken … driftwood

Amid a sea of depression, hurt, and suicidal seaweed

My life is beginning to concede

Suicide has been decreed

Dipped in my thoughts daily

Force feed

It's a total impede of my survival

Indeed

I don't want suicide to succeed

So this writing I reread

I try to pay heed

To the damaging thoughts my brain suffers

I'm guessing they antecede the act

The death-defying or overtrying act

If the fight is over

The stampede

Will proceed, and death is guaranteed

There's a waiver in my handwriting

Depression I'm highlighting

There's been another sighting

All my inner strength I'm uniting

But the thoughts of living are uninviting

I'm so trying to win with this writing

Stop my brain bullfighting with depression

FFS its back in session

Three weeks in a hotel room

Has nurtured depression's gloom

I'm worried everyone will see

Depression's showroom

Wearing a suicidal costume

Depression the bride

Suicide the groom, wearing a neck rope perfume

Scented of death and release entomb

Who's the chairman?

This is depression's boardroom

Come on in, there's room

Suicide boom

Will you leave an heirloom?

Would your death reach the newsroom?

If I ask for help I feel I'm grassing

Surpassing the chin up, chest out, amassing

I think depression is trespassing

What do you think?

I'm just asking;

Don't want a verbal blasting

This thought process is cracking, massive, slashing, and holding

A casting, leading role

Suicide assassin

Ready to unfasten your soul

There's no compassion

That's depression's goal

If unchecked it's out of control

Take your life like two points

NFL field goal

I'm looking for the loophole

I used to be so rock and roll

A somebody

A someone

Somebody's somebody

I'm heading towards suicide's door

Dead body

They'll send me to Coventry

I used to be so bubbly

I was handed a marriage redundancy

Uncharted territory

I entered melancholy

Lost my trust company

In fact I was bent over and fucked doggy, animal husbandry

Did you get fucked on your hen party?

Embalm my body

I trusted wholly

And in front of God you were unholy

Slowly

Your hate for me grew

E. coli

Now I'm suffering

Depression, suicide, anxiety -wrapped ravioli

I've never been so lowly

Or lonely

I've lost my team

I'm just left with my goalie

While I was married

I got too cosy

Can a suicide be low key?

I know there's no trophy

Only a fucked-up ceremony

Depression and death, matrimony

This book is my testimony

Don't deserve a ceremony

I'm still heartbroken

Slipped into a depression coma

Can't control my emotions

I play through my suicide

Slow motion

Again on the suicide locomotive

Full steam ahead

I can't control my head

But I have a superstitious notion

That self-dead people are loathed

And the door to heaven will be closed

Left in hell to decompose

Demonized

To do what he did was he hypnotized?

His depression was so well disguised

He didn't advertise

Being tough and silent were standardized

I'm telling you, though, if unsupervised

Depression becomes franchised

And sells to death

Then life becomes disenfranchised

Against this mind … Fuck

I want to be immunized

I want to tell my family, but I'm scared

I'll be chastised, not advised

Other than the emphasized

Chin up, chest out

Why are you stressed out?

Depression

Dispel the doubt

But I'm in a new bout

And my good is being edged out

Yesterday's yesterday

I contemplated ending my pain

All alone I lay debating

With my suicidal thoughts

The repercussions I'd be creating

It's been accumulating

My life force is evaporating

All from my divorce this originated

I feel my treatment has been unregulated

I fucking need to be rehabilitated

Deep breaths, L.J.P

Become oxygenated

Depression and crew are manipulating

They have you incarcerated

Infuriated and infatuated with their option

Pain release

You're titillated with self-termination

Depression knows it will be implicated

But in this state of mind, you're fascinated

Show me a way that isn't outdated

There's a rope; make a noose, it's been baited

Where would it be located?

Must be elevated

Don't want any hesitating

Remember you'll be suffocating

Unventilated

Wasted

Cheated

Suicide greeted

Depression's mission completed

Your life is defeated

You'll be completely deleted

Have you been maltreated?

Jesus, man up

But I'm isolated totally deflated

Taking a self-inflicted beating

I wasn't cheating

I was excreted when my time was completed

Now two years on

I'm untreated

Knocking on hell's big door

Not yet admitted

I'm holding my hands up, scared to proceed

Not something I want to succeed in

I wish this last four years could be deleted

Never again to be repeated

Shit don't let me transgress

Not gonna lie, I'm in a depression distress

Nearly to excess

None the less

I'm trying to suppress

How are you? my friends will ask

Ok I reply in a freeway horseplay

But ok is bang in the middle of br*ok*en

My words are still choking, depression stowaway

Fucks my ok

Like I'm on death row

Life wears away

Will I be alone next Valentine's Day?

My delicate mind exponential decay

It's underway, rapid beating

Depression's mass meeting

History repeating

D asks for trust; put it here

Suicidal safekeeping

We will bring it out later

For another battering

Suicide badgering

Please keep battling

You're on your own

Taking a mental battering

This is now a returning problem

But I'm not able to start bantering

If I'm honest, it's fucking shattering

Can't properly sleep

My fucked-up mind is chattering

Constantly clattering

Depression is in there constantly plastering

Suicides follow-me guide

Manufacturing a take-your-life approach

A fuck-it-all-kill yourself coach

Use a rabbit snare become suicide poached

Cutthroat

Anxieties attacking now, gunboat

Looking for the casting vote

I asked before

Depression antidote

Help me; I need a suicide defence

Torpedo boat

I'm scared this life is going to get outvoted

I know I'm outnumbered

Never normally outgunned

But I'm scared I'll succumb

To this constant suicide hum

WTF have I become?

I'm looking at a nightmare outcome

Rule of thumb

With your income should be banging

The happy steel drum

Shake your brain

Overcome,

Overcome,

Overcome

Rusty depression brake drum

Lube it up, Jamaican rum

Do you have unearned income?

This situation is like a comic book

Depression = Arch-rival

Suicide = Rival's side-kick

You gotta start swinging for your own survival

You need a revival

What's the time of arrival?

But still a blood rage

I'm self-homicidal

Depression disciple

It's testing my mortality

Suicide is becoming not an abnormality

But a commonality

Daily dream I'm a fatality

Cult of personality

Individuality

Heterosexuality

I'm hiding multiple personalities

With no rationality

Currently suicide punctuality is shitty

Trying spirituality to defeat

Depressive mind brutality

I need solidarity

Neutrality

I've lost my vitality, sexuality, split personality

Depression—I've been swallowed "Jonah"

Kill myself—hematoma

Soda Stream—Suicide flavour

I've become a fucking loner

Loneliness carcinoma

I'm in year four of this suicide diploma

I've been lucky

Malignant melanoma

Cancer-like depression

Eats your good cells

Rounds them up like Mexican cartels

I don't care what you say, there are parallels

Death cells either route

I'm not totally immune

Depression has passed my barrage balloons

Too soon

Heading towards a Suicidal honeymoon

Slice your wrist

What, this phase of the moon?

Get drunk and do it

Animated cartoon

You want to go to heaven on a meteorological balloon

Spat out like a suicidal buffoon

Tin spittoon

Maybe these feelings are back

It is a new moon

So I just hide in my hotel room

Will it be the place I die?

Suicide cell

All is well I will continue to tell

While I dwell in my despair

Not even lifted a single barbell

My physical being is also being beaten

Depression raising hell

Crossbow and apple

William Tell

Opinion yell … me

Yes or no, what do I do?

Well shake your head and keep it in

Came from a friend

An older civilian

I could tell he was uncomfortable with my suicidal theorem

Then tried to pass on his depression wisdom

When he left, I cried

Because I had tried

I was bereft

I opened my broken soul … I confessed

Now I realise it was too much for him

His exit … stage left

That was my old people's screen test

As I write this down, I remember I enlightened eight of my friends

We entered my mind's wild west

A problem shared is a problem halved

What a laugh

Judgement of what you tell them

I could see it

It was telegraphed across their faces

Paragraph after paragraph

Hearing my suicidal subsections

I could see some rejection

Thinking you're mad in the head

Depression direction

Marriage recollections

Broken down sections

Forget that cunt—redemption required

Suicide is on a manhunt

Trying to confront all that you are

It's a cold front and currently depression

Is out in front

Winning the survival treasure hunt

Come on L. J. P., give life a punt

Become less antiquated

What you mean, current?

I'm sorry; I've been burnt

And through my pain I've learnt

Being on my own will always have a suicidal undercurrent

It's become the normal

Formal view of abnormal

I know it's fucking awful

I'm in Milan, trying to work

But I've become an insomniac, nocturnal

Depression sent in its probing thoughts

Suicidal Lieutenant Colonel

Spouting kill yourself waffle

It stinks so bad

Rotten offal

In Switzerland assisted suicide

Is lawful and legitimate

I could get excited about that, wax lyrical

Death admissible

Insignificant suicide

I'm under mind arrest

False imprisonment

Not a willing participant

These thoughts are becoming significant

Depression is thinking magnificent

Proposing a suicidal incident

I'm asking politely, What's the etiquette?

What must I implement?

I'm not sure any technique I could simulate

I mean suicide practice

Estimate

I so want to articulate

A mind's that intricate

Delicately illiterate

To emotions I must express

It's not insignificant

I need a verbalized instrument

To yell out this incident

All the time being vigilant to suicide

Dissident

Thoughts like I have

Predicament

Most are innocent survival

Majority are sickening suicide

Toss a coin; let fate decide

Run and hide

You're a survival contestant

Be an objector to death

A deflector, a self-protector

Your life's managing director

A terrible thought's interceptor

Don't let them in your sector

All my inner pain says except her

Except her what

Adultery

I find it hard, all of this skulduggery

It's impeding my recovery

Shock charge my mind—car battery

No bitter taste—just celery, it's watery

But my mind remains troubled

Encased

Thundery

Depression released

It's unleashed

Brutal mind thuggery

Don't play the suicide lottery

It's a tough calculation

You'll always lose

Life amputation

Her fornication

Created this downward mobilization

It's an uncharted navigation

Depression and crew

Orchestrated

Come on, man

Shake your head

Become reincarnated before you die

It's just a mind ulceration

Clogged up mental vegetation

Please get better, accentuation

Don't join the asphyxiation association

I'm not giving you authorization

You don't have the documentation

Don't want an immediate verbal ejaculation

Not all will understand your death's aspiration

They'll think you're talking defecation

You'll be back in desolation

Undressing depression's dissertation

Trying to delay its detonation

Don't get a first

Increased desperation

But your mind's already impregnated

Isolated

Inundated, feels death-obligated

Hand in your notice

Check out

Life designated

As I write this down, suffocated

Violated

Waiting to be annihilated

Bastardization of my mind

It's a feeling I have all the time

Pump me with some healing juice

Cannulation

I'll give you cooperation

Gain some accreditations

I beat depression —decoration

But still hiding in desperation

I said it before, I'm screaming for help but only to me

I realise I'm suffering

I'm declining

An infestation of pain

Now my head's insulation

It's so fucking inhuman

I'm too pumped to try meditation

I'm going through a mind fuck time

Depression molestation

Not again

Deep breath, palpitation

I feel my life is now on suicide probation

I thought I was in a mind-state stagnation

It's all fucking with my vocation

I'm being mentally exploited and being away it's being accelerated

All for depression's gratification—your

Humiliation

Incrimination

Suicide qualification

Do it in Milan

That's a tough repatriation

Refrigeration

Back to the English nation

Don't want to die alone

But I struggle to use the phone

Who … who … who do I tell

That nearly every morning, noon, and night

I'm in a suicidal fight?

People live in a problem-free zone

It's a no go

Someone come be my chaperone

I need help

Open my occipital bone

Let me see

Shake your neck, your head

Release some testosterone

Grow a backbone

Don't fall into depression's drop zone

Change your clock

Suicide time zone

These thoughts are overblown

Don't let this become depression's abode

This is now another episode

Install a mind-dial telephone

No fuck it, a megaphone

Don't suppress your cries

You need to express your distress

This is an inner peace request

Nevertheless

The pain, it holds me restrained

Dealing with depression I'm untrained

I need it explained

I just keep it self-contained

Where? Alone in my thoughts

Depression, anxiety, and suicide

Are unrestrained

Free to roam

I wish I was at home

But not my gaff

The emptiness is unexplained

This depression is definitely becoming ingrained

And I'm creating a feeling

That all my relationships are strained

Well that's just hare-brained

But it keeps depression entertained

Its schedule unchanged

And unashamed

But outwardly

I must keep it unnamed, restrained

Subdued and muted

Handcuffed, totally fettered

This feeling must be bettered

I'm depression dictated

A prisoner who's alive to the outside

But mind is depression guarded

German Shepherd, suicidal tethered

Clever depression

Again the aggressor

At your leisure

I'm an unwilling member

Don't want the T-shirt, sweater; I want to get better

Release this head fuck

The high pressure

Altogether, altogether depression displeasure

If you live in the now

Pleasure checker-double-decker

Keep up your pecker

Depression's chancellor of the exchequer

Do I make this a newsletter

Or go one better

Depression's determination letter?

All that equals

Is a condolence gazette, token effort

Suicide, anxiety, depression baguette

I'll have a sad burger

Go light on the sorrow

It could be the launching pad

Make me a suicidal Olympian

I did think actually

Would I be scantily clad

As I rode into suicide battle

Sir Galahad

Jousting my demons?

I'm trying not to go bad

But I wander my mind's fucked plains

Suicidal nomad,

Nomad

No

Mad

I think I'm gonna go bad

Stop operating or functioning alive

Suicide is summoning

And I'm stumbling

Struggling

Depression

Is guzzling, bloodsucking

If I told you I'm depressed I'd get a tongue lashing

Help, I'm malfunctioning

Dysfunctional, troubling

I feel I should be grovelling

My mind needs buttressing

Supporting

Someone please come rushing

But nothing

You can't help someone who doesn't want help

But you might be the first step

To help empower

Change that person's brainpower

Up the horsepower

Help them devour despair

Gulp down anxiety

And starve suicidal tendencies

Engorge their good

Regurgitate a positive mind state

Engrave survivor on their nameplate

Assist to remove the depression head roommate

Make a positive buzzing sound—bombilate

Start the eviction notice—depopulate

Commiserate as we decapitate

This sad mental state

Suicide— anxiety — depression

Be gone

Want me to elaborate?

Okay, demon, fuck off

Be gone

Is it a werewolf? Shoot it

Bang

Silver nitrate

What is the current suicidal turnover rate?

I wonder with how many I relate

I know we have an internal pain

Probably similar contamination

Fucking our rehabilitation

What is the suicide mortality rate?

Has it been backdated?

All the names on it met?

Depression— anxiety — suicide … checkmate

I wish that part could just be amputated

The more I suffer I realise

It's all correlated

Pain, suffering, and depression cooperate

They fuck with your good

It will slowly dissipate

There's an uncontrolled death rate

Mental health unstable

Open the floodgate

Depression is on the hunt— suicide predate

Hell's doors are open, offering a discounted rate

But in this mindset it's tough

Suicides though can't be controlled; they just germinate

Sprout

Early shoot

Sprouting Suicide inside your mind

It doesn't consider the mind's intellect

Suicide doesn't need no IQ level

Once it's taken hold

Screw you

Meet the devil

Depression doesn't want you to come through

Needs you to sip some suicidal homebrew

And then fall through

Become subdued

And follow this suicide taboo

Let's be honest

Kill yourself

There's a lot to live up to

Don't get depression's message wrong, misconstrued

It's a hard thing to do

Upside down steel U-shaped

Unlucky horseshoe

Make a test run, sneak preview

If you do kill yourself

For so many it would be a death

Out of the blue

Only a few are inside the loop

But I promised I'm okay

Not lied yet and jumped without a chute

Took that swan dive—not yet

Only depression, anxiety, and suicide

Would be elated

If someone read this text

How would it be translated?

Would they be captivated

Nauseated

Or intimidated?

I'd hope they'd give me some help

Make it advocated

Pushed forward

Not feel daunted

Scared or deterred

People understand my vision is blurred

Depression—Curse word

Anxiety —Can't be heard

Suicide—A watchword

But it's never heard until it's been spurred on to take

A poor soul to the noose gallows

Neck break

Mental health needs assistance

You got a screw loose, head brake

Need to be quicker on the uptake

But depression gets stuck in your mind

Like a river flow

Oxbow Lake

Trapped in brain matter the devil's food cake

I'll keep screaming

Please someone hit the emergency brake

FFS

Depression is now in top gear

Outside lane, close to overtake

It all started from your heartache

This suicidal outbreak

If people knew—screw loose—fruitcake

Give your fucking head a shake

I hear you, snowflake

But depression is now fully awake

It's smothering my good, like a biscuit covered with cream topping

Cheesecake

And I do pray each night I see daybreak

Well that's maybe a lie

I'm always awake

Along with my depression body hurts—backache

Topping yourself, let's be honest

Is a huge thing to undertake and what if …

It was a mistake

Noose tightens … oh fuck it … too late

But daily depression builds sick headache

Waiting to strike … coiled rattlesnake

Some days I know it's a mistake

I ensure that I always hesitate

And try not to translate the depressive message I receive

Not to fixate on the suicide release debate

I really do try to appreciate and contemplate

All that I have to celebrate

At points I understand it's insane

But depression and its crew

Are in charge, dictate

Puts me in dismay

I realise my life is in danger

And every day is my mental battle—6 June

D-day

Groundhog,

Groundhog

It's a mental slog

Clouded, thick, mental smog

Polluted and evil

Suicide is suited and booted

And ready to remain

The undisputed

Killer of men thirty to forty-five

Not many survive

They become depression executed

Maybe some get lucky … just wounded

But let's not fuck about depression is ruthless

But music, writing, and people are therapeutic

Must destroy depression pre-embryotic

Close your eye = pupil myopic

Your head's full of shit

Beginning emotional purging

Psychotherapeutic—go see the doctor

Am I better yet? Bluetick

Hide in the appointment, don't tell too much

Can't let them see I'm too sick

In and out, damn that was quick

Keep off the bottle L. J. P.—sobriety

Don't mention anxiety in front of society

You'll get judged, majority that's it—insanity

Only a few will have true loyalty

It's why the issue is held privately

In privacy

Quietly in fact silently

And that's the irony

Talk and let it out; unleash the gravity

And finally, in all its entirety, help release some pressure

Ease your mentality

I've become antisocial

Absconded from life

Deprived, love starved

Developed OCD

Not obsessive-compulsive disorder

Over Controlling depression

Is on order,

Order,

Order

The chair of the house screams remain seated

Houses of Parliament

Your whole body is being mistreated

Don't open up, become suicidal

Satan greeted

Worship at his feet

But discretion please

Don't beep-beep the horn

Keep it low key

Only on your death day will your OCD be exposed

Until then remain composed

And keep your detailed depression enclosed

And at the point its exposed

Your broken heartbeat will be foreclosed

Shut up shop

Give your wrist an almighty chop

Depression, anxiety don't want you to stop

You're entering a suicidal sweet shop

With the devil whispering, 'Do it'

It'll be neat

When we meet

In hell's own fire—coward

Feel the heat.

Can you feel the heat?

Stripping your soul

It's no mean feat

As you cut in slow, blood flow

Dripping

While your gripping

Onto what you once had

You're now a depression dunce

Go stand in the corner

That's right, cunt boy

Be your own suicide mourner

Don't worry, fucker

In hell it will be warmer

You're now a suicide adorer

With depression and anxiety

You're judge, jury, and executioner

That rope on my neck

Please add a softener

Loosen it please

I read you survive in my stars

Astrologer

I'm a revolutionary

Prisoner of Alcatraz

The escapee

Let's die with some pizzazz

I'll give you the visual

The spectacular

My mind keeps hitting the bar

It's not straight thoughts

It's gone peculiar

Angular

I'm looking for a rope to become my unacceptable strangler

I'll happily become a dangler

On my way to the wooden box

Rectangular

To control these thoughts I need a cowboy

A depression wrangler

A flag-draped individual

Star-spangled banner

I've become a social abstainer

I was not a remainer

Complete leaver

Wide receiver

I'm now a depression believer

How many would be grievers?

Hands up

Let me see

But I'm not openly asking you to see

Remember depression

Keeps this with me

And only me

My mind is in session

Well it's in trouble

Get some help on the double

Left, right. Left, right

You'll be all right

Fuck you gave us a fright

Well for a long time now I've been losing this fight

And my life wants to take flight

Fly off a tree

Only the rope on my neck to stop my descent

I've already descended into the dark

Doom and a constant haze of gloom

Anxiety AND depression dance a quick step

Glitterball suicide ballroom

Do I give off the persona, suicidal emitter?

I try not to, peeps

I should shimmer

To everyone a huge white-teeth grinner

This stress eating is not making me thinner

I should be slimmer

Someone

Something show me a sign

A signal, some type of glimmer

Garden my bad brain, do the borders

Petrol— depression's Strimmer

The thoughts I'm suffering— depression's delivery

Invasion of privacy

Depression's dynasty

Signing up … unadvisedly

Privately I'm fighting this mental rivalry

If I lose this battle my body will be lifelessly silent

These thoughts are now violent

Depression is suicide's pilot

All-conquering

Rampaging

A mental tyrant

Take my thoughts abroad claim asylum

Be in depression denial

Can't see no cure on the horizon

No fuck it, L. J. P., you're suicidal

Solemn

Stood on top of the swan dive column

On the way down do the suicide slalom

As you hit the bottom

Become crestfallen

Lose your problems

Can anyone help

Wrap my head in cotton?

Cotton,

Cotton

Cotton wool protection

My head's full of imperfections

There's a distinct disconnection

A positive misdirection

Give my head a depression caesarean

Remove this fungal infection

Depression house of correction

Change anxiety's angle of reflection

It entered my Mary and Joseph Stable

Immaculate conception

People will start to see my pain

I can't hide my visual perception

Need to change my life's path

Its goal, its direction

My inner feelings not ready for rejection

Outwardly overcorrecting my I'm okay projection

To all that I meet

I offer a hidden depression greet

Whilst every Friday I fill in a timesheet

I so want redemption

But I'm finding my thoughts have exemption

They have me on a kill yourself direction

I want to tell people

But fear rejection

It builds apprehension

I need a mind bodyguard to help strengthen

I'm trying not to bitch around my depression

But it's pushing me hard

Promoting

Suicidal pitch

Trying to give me a life disconnect

Tow bar unhitched

Run hard handspring swan dive

Golden death's bridge

Land in the drink below

Water witch

What a bitch

Don't unload your issues

You fucking snitch

Running your mouth off

Overspill

Irrigation ditch

But I need to denounce depression

Be profound in my approach

Don't get depression impounded

It's nothing to be astounded by

Just bounce on by death's open door

It's priming to pounce with anxiety

Propping the threshold preventer

Holding the doorknob

Excited to give your life an incredibly dangerous shove

Get you to inhale the suicide spores

Unleash the fury

Release the gore

If you succeed there won't be no encore

I need a volunteer

Be my mentor

Today I feel on an upward relief

I've not been sat deep in my divorce grief

Head's been busy

Completely work thinking

But suicidal thoughts are still lingering

Their mingling, underlying

Simmering

Constantly whispering

Depression delivering

And I can't lie; I've been suicidal, death picturing

Increased considering

But the fact I'm still here … bewildering

In fact it's staggering

I've been alone battling

Grappling

Building a defensive wall

Scaffolding

Hoping for depression dismantling

Deconstructing

I go to work with a lost zest

Just an office mannequin

Really struggling with chattering

Expecting my head to be splattering

No open coffin; it won't be flattering

Mind's gone baby-like, teething ring

I had a life dream—Martin Luther King

Deepens depression's descent, manufacturing,

Manufacturing a maddening mind map

Remember suicides sat-nav

Feel well for a day

Fuck it just a stop gap

The way I've developed

I think it's a handicap

I daydream of shooting kneecaps

Everyone's … you okay L. J.P.?

Backslap, smile, a hug, it's all a lie

I still seek a deadly mishap

Or just a natural heart attack

I'm a mentally handicapped maniac

With a good mind so far off track

Thoughts so dark they cloud my mind

Tooth plaque

It's a constant head fuck lookout; stand back

Tracks 1 to 10 suicidal soundtrack

My thoughts ain't right

It's not so straightforward anymore

Gone dark, carbon-black

This is all this white man's burden

I'm fighting to stay behind the safety curtain

I thought I was tough Spartan,

Spartan power,

Spartan fight,

Spartan ha jokes

More like a mind botanical garden

Head full of depression toxins

Dioxins

Need some blood-clotting brain action

Thromboxane

In need of defensive formations

Is there a life's auction

To buy the survival?

I beg for a mental revival

When's it coming

Time of arrival?

Still depression denial

Scared of reprisal if I spiral to death's door

On a one-wheel suicidal unicycle

But I'm not clowning around

I'm counting down

Discounting drowning

Mind keeps clouding

Thousand ways to die

But I'm currently too shy

To say goodbye

But that thought is always nearby

Right there is my mind's eye,

Mind's eye

Bye-bye

It pictures I die

It takes nothing to cry

My marriage was a snide

Depression is now astride my chest

Not letting me rest

I need it to be purified

Suicide set aside

I'm terrified

To testify

I'm terrified

I'm gonna die depression by side

With no one by my side

A lonely, satisfied self-homicide

I tell my mind, *Come on FFS*

Toe the line

Behave, obey, heed what I say

Ride the white steed

Don't let suicide succeed

I constantly hide in my deep-ingrained depression

I'm starting to believe it's totally right that mind's in a fight

It's contrasting

Between the dark and the light

Which side is outlasting?

Who knows for sure?

Outstanding

Still I'm screaming

While depression is calculating

Eeny, meeny, miny, moe

Got depression by the throat

But his corner is stronger

I arrived in a survival woolly coat, cashmere

Back toe to toe suicidal recital

Surviving, enduring, holding on

Striving for survival

Devising a depression deferral

Rising, shining, trying so hard, not hiding … liar

Hiding has become my hobby still isolated

You mention suicide people become ignorant and rude ... snobby

Scared you mean dead body

Snobby about suicide

May as well be talking Punjabi

So keep it in my depression head lobby

Wear that smile; I'm a happy zombie

Scared my neck will do the old Okie Chokie

Slip off the chair

Outcome unclear

I'm sure it will pinch

Life to death transfer complete.

Life left hanging, slipping away

Death's car doors opened

Depression chauffeur

Holding the revolver

Silencer

A depression balancer

Catastrophic calendar

Slide into the devil's den

He's the proprietor

The original manager

He's been tweaking those depression rioters

They have the suicidal cocktail primed

Molotov destruction

Firebomb your good mind

Qualms passed my mind

Vomit reaction

Suicidal squeamishness

I'm admitting I'm depressed

This word game I hope is redeeming us!

I realise my mind is crossing unevenness

Seasickness

Suicide's key witness

How'd I treat this illness

Freeing us

Teaching us?

I'm stuck with a strict chin up Britishness

All the time depression and crew are teasing us

To them routine business

To deceive us … suicide meaningless

We all witness depression goading us

Extreme wickedness

Help me, show willingness

Don't want to be suicidal infamous

Depression carcinomas

Thoughts of death frivolous

But really full of spitefulness

Wickedness

With growing vividness of my dramatic dreams

Screaming underwater where all others are oblivious

Hospitable is my mind to some … fix

But depression keeps opening its bag of fucking tricks …

I'm holding them off … Crucifix

Taking any quick fix

Depression, anxiety smothered salt and vinegar

Wrapped in yesterday's newspaper

Fish and chips

A fucking, weeping tea

Chipping away at sanity

Apocalypse

Brick by brick

I'm just a poor sad soul

Grasping

Holding

Onto some form of life … existence

But I'm feeling resistance

A complete resistance from a life surrounded

It's bounded

It's wagons hailed from the outside attackers

Must constrain the attack

Fucking fight back

Why can't I rewrite and upload a new will to fight

I'd even meet you at the battle hill

First daylight

But honesty of my depressed head I'm struggling

Can't be in the limelight

I keep getting suicidal stage fright

Which is great as no hindsight after that rope becomes tight,

Tight,

Tight

Face it right

Face it … sunlight

Sunlight helps

Cancel that subscription

Suicide ain't right

Don't call me suicidal

It's exhausting

Bloody daunting

All helped with this silent talking

I need releasing … pay the ransom

Hostage depressed

Depressed hostage

Suicide wastage

Unwanted

A daily survival forage

Count your losses and gallop towards your Saviour

Sanity horses of colossus

Thank fuck you've got an enormous subconscious

Have you got the nerve?

Hypothalamus

Broken vows, promises

St Michael's Church

Hand on the Bible

Bridal betrayal

Now my life is stifled

Muffled

It's idle

Anxiety guzzled

I need to scream for help, but I'm muzzled

I'm ruffled

And I'm realizing I'm in trouble …

As I continue to struggle

Anxiety has more hustle

I'm dragging my knuckles

As I shuffle from day to day

Trying not to kick the bucket

Become untroubled

On the double

I need my life tranquil

Smuggled in sanctum

Past depression's guard

I need to be thankful

Dismantle depression

I'm sure I could handle

Talking survival language

We never crossed a word

But the silence we shared can't be taken back

If I said hello, would you ignore me and send me another blow?

If you needed to hit me, I'd give you a free throw

An open blow

I'd just hold my breath for a borrowed second, inflow

Twice this week I've glimpsed you close

Dreams are so real you tiptoed through

I woke knowing you'd been; you left an afterglow …

You were my Promised Land, Rose of Jericho

Then I realised I'd wandered into my Suicidal Skid Row

All I wanted was you at the end of the rainbow

Pot of gold

But I realise that was so long ago

I have to let go …

How though? This is my status quo

I stand alone; it isn't well known

The love that I fight

The love of myself; I detest what I've become

Highest achievement suicide scum

How is it overcome?

I tell anyone who listens that I don't want you

You're dead to me

But you won't leave me a constant niggle

Unhappy outcome

My head's gone brittle

Grim reaper's coming

Hammer and sickle

Commit suicide; it's your committal

Daily reminders hurt my soul

I became your second fiddle

Heading mental hospital

Little by little

I'm losing any part of L. J. P. I have left

What you see isn't me …

Again I'm bereft

But you're all unaware

Tread carefully, beware

And I'm hurt more than I show

All of the time my life is grieving

I'm conceding I'm in a depression, misleading

I outwardly express a happiness glow

To anyone who cares …

Who cares?

Who cares wins

Bravo zero two suicide's

Suicidal skins

Unaware of the pain

It's insane

I wish I was walking in the air

Not swinging

I need reasonable care

Deep in my mind psychological warfare

Lord help me fight

I'll go to morning prayer

Get me out of this nightmare

It's a constant kill yourself fanfare

Electric chair

My defences are threadbare

I'm not in self-pity

It's just unfair

I can't see it

Does anyone actually care?

Cos I don't feel it, I swear

Trying to keep out of despair

Straight out of nowhere

So I act so debonair

Chipper

A happy day tripper

A secret suicidal sightseer

Locked in my mind prisoner of war

I'm hiding multiple scars, hidden tears; my life is in arrears

Help me before it disappears

I need a mind Band Aid to hide my fears

Help me reappear

2020, please be a good year

I ask this, and I'm being sincere

I've put on my mental armour

An anti- depression veneer

Inside my head it's a clearer atmosphere

Depression's been pushed south

A different hemisphere.

A daily battle that I'm currently winning

Rumble in the jungle, deep depths Mozambique!

I'd become scared I was a depression freak

My will had become weak, meek, afraid to speak.

But thank God currently depression is an ageing antique

I'm disposing slowly of my

Depression, anxiety, and the be afraid idea

So to speak

I'm cooking on gas bubble and squeak

Can't wait to be fully back on track, including my physique

I've developed a helpful technique

Engaged and disposing of depression, soon obsolete

So happy deep inside that living life can be a reality

I'm on a revival, extreme survival, emotional elite

But I still keep my old thoughts discreet

Admitting I have had a depression routine

I know I'll be judged to the extreme.

And if I'm not feeling great, my thoughts will be on a balance beam

Three months ago my life of happiness was a pipe dream

I was screaming to be redeemed

I needed to let off steam

I've created a survival scheme

Revival regime

Just for your knowledge

I never prayed on the Bible

My mind was so tidal

Completely in deep water; remember, I was suicidal

Self-homicidal

In that time my thoughts were unrivalled

Depression versus good a total mismatch

My life because of depression was being attacked.

Demon thoughts were being hatched

They became attached

Unwillingly connected

But depression was so committed

Good side's defence was constricted

Only way out was writing and depicting my depression

The pain that flowed out to these pages was unrestricted

Depression was so keen to keep me suicidal addicted

Pain on an hourly basis, suffering, afflicted

The suffering was depression -scripted

Sense of right was disconnected

I was stricken

A depression victim

Suicidal sickness

Truly felt my body was infected

But I'm now pushing back

Depression rejected

No longer suicidal, that's been disconnected

I was so dejected, self-neglected

I became socially unconnected

Disoriented, felt my life was wretched

Regretted I thought I couldn't ask for help

I became tormented

Depression-filled … dejected

I feel my days are powering strong

It won't be too long before

L. J. P. is completely depression -free

It becomes a life deportee

Can start to report that I'm no longer worrying about being a divorcee

Still not looking for love; it's like I've become an emotional vaccine

Non-loving, I was depressive

It's my idiosyncrasy

Can't settle down; static built up in my head

Atmospheric electricity

Needed space and time

Theory of relativity

Dealing with depression

This written account helped me brilliantly

The results didn't come instantly

It started off so miserably

But helped me prevent my suicidal sympathy

At the time I didn't realise that it was my irresponsibility

I nearly let depression win this battle

Suicidal self-sufficiency, skilfully sidestepped that disaster

Dropped depression the shoulder

Now feeling so much bolder

A proud householder

My own life survivalist, I bought in; I'm a stakeholder

I've nearly cracked it, this depression decoder

It was a brain-fucking freeloader

Mental mind game … poker

Anxiety and depression became the suicidal promoter

Luckily I stayed straight, sober, a complete non-smoker

And this closed opening up I'm completing

Is my depression disclosure

Now I have it in its own enclosure

Surrounded, pounded, and now I'm totally astounded

No longer feel abandoned

I'm looking forwards; my mind has expanded

My good mind has been depression unbounded.

So I was

Free-falling through days

I lived in a total depression daze

As I wandered through my mentally muddled mind maze

My will to die young now been set ablaze

I was heading edgeways …

Those weren't the good old days …

I didn't know I was sick

And I struggled to come to terms with it and admit …

But I realised something was wrong; I was living my life a lie

Counterfeit

I was full steam ahead crazy batshit, sat in the unconscious depression cockpit

Not being able to talk out loud, I felt such a hypocrite

You said it, I wanted to disappear but was living in fear

The emotional issue that I had developed

Came with some scary conditions

Depression, and suicide

Were my daily hot topics

But luckily for my life I learnt to write it out

I let all my built-up feelings flow out

And from that free writing here it is the emergence

My depression escape this is my egress

I no longer feel worthless

With some eagerness I want to survive and push forward

And thankfully I don't feel no vengeance

I'm going to become a goodwill servant

I want to help others; I'll be their deterrent

Help other people remove a mind fuck burden

I'm moving forwards now I have a purpose

Let me help you live; I'll be your life merchant

Talk you into buying your right to live

Be positively active

Don't be depression smothered

As I fly so high

Selfishly I feel flamboyant

I'm on my way home

Heart is aching, can't wait

Happy, happy … fuck, I think that I'm actually happy

A feeling that has truly alluded me

I've been depression deluded

Confused

Thought my life was a ruse

But I've developed a schedule

I needed a schedule, redirection

A nine to five to keep my mind in line

It was running out of time

Thought it was my time … but I survived

Depression was any cat-'o-nine-tails

I was silently wailing; I was screaming

My inner being had lost all its feelings

As I battled on all fronts

Let's all be honest, depression is a cunt

I've been free for some time, but I know it's in my life underlying

But I've been totally defiant

Fighting, thriving, scrambling to survive

I've been determined suicide won't rule my life

A depression normality = brutality

As I couldn't focus on a normal life

The way I was going I was in complete strife

I couldn't take more heartache

There's nothing left there to break

Sadly I now realise

Giving all my unconditional love was a huge mistake

An act in time I wish I could remake

For fuck sake

The decisions you make will guide your life and your heartbreak

Should never live with regret, some philosopher once stated

Ensure your thoughts are repopulated … adjusted … corrected

Fear I'll live alone, die alone won't open up to any person

You know why now; I'm defensive, guarded

Because I was disregarded

How will I trust again? Fuck knows it's alarming

I don't think I could handle the mental torture

Biggest thing I've learnt through all of this drama

And now is my number one mantra …

Don't marry if one of you is unsure !

It will makes your life simpler.

The end

But not the end of L. J. P.

I'm so happy to report

I'm just getting started.

What you've just read prevented me from being self-terminated.

Can't believe I'd be dead, deleted.

Depression, suicide with its be afraid anxiety have fucked off and left.

And that is for the best.

L. J. P.

Keep on kicking.

Printed in the United States
By Bookmasters